FARMS

GREAT PLACES TO VISIT

Jason Cooper

The Rourke Corporation, Inc.
Vero Beach, Florida 32964

Edited by Sandra A. Robinson

PHOTO CREDITS
© Lynn M. Stone: All photos

ACKNOWLEDGEMENTS
The author thanks Marion Behling, Carol Boesche, Becky and
Sarah Rosenwinkel, and Gatorama (Palmdale, FL) for their
cooperation in the preparation of this book

LIBRARY OF CONGRESS
Library of Congress Cataloging-in-Publication Data
Cooper, Jason, 1942-
  Farms / by Jason Cooper.
  p. cm. — (Great places to visit)
  Includes index.
  Summary: Briefly describes what goes on at various kinds of
farms: horse farms, dairy farms, crop farms, and others.
  ISBN 0-86593-211-5
  1. Farms—Juvenile literature. [1. Farms.] I. Title.
II. Series: Cooper, Jason, 1942- Great places to visit.
S519.C63 1992
630—dc20   92-10078
                        CIP
                        AC

TABLE OF CONTENTS

FARMS

You will see something very important when you visit a farm—America's food supply!

Farms are the places where **domestic** animals, like cattle and pigs, and food **crops,** like grain and vegetables, are raised.

Farms may be a few acres in size or thousands of acres. Large farms, especially those where cattle are raised, are called **ranches.**

Guernsey dairy cattle on a
Midwestern farm

LIFE ON THE FARM

Farmers are the people who live and work on farms. Farmers often work long hours, sometimes in the darkness of night or early morning.

Most farmers use machines to plow and plant fields and to harvest crops each fall.

Farmers also have to take care of their animals and keep their tractors, harrows, **combines** and other machines working well.

Time for milking in a dairy barn

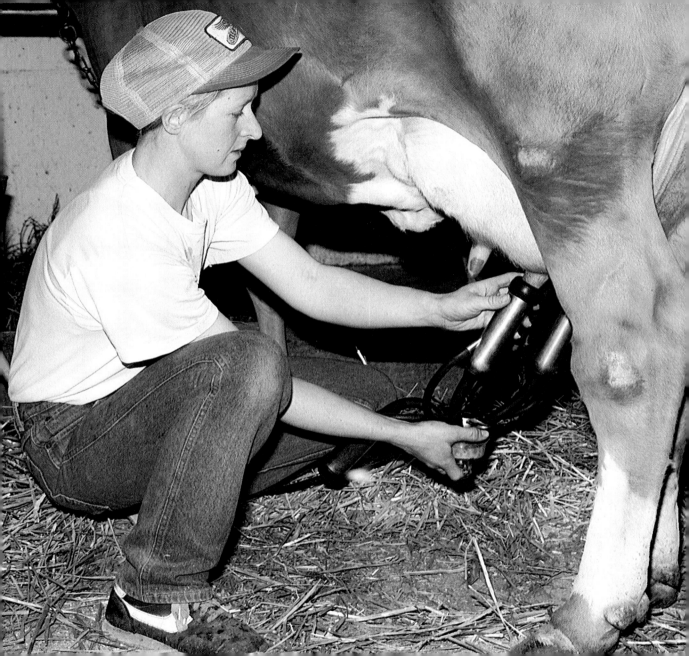

FARMS FOR BEEF, PORK AND LAMB

Nearly half of American farms raise **livestock**—beef cattle, hogs or sheep.

Beef cattle are raised for food rather than for milk. Hogs, or pigs, are raised for their meat (pork) and for other purposes. Their hair, for example, is used for brushes.

Sheep are raised for meat (mutton and lamb) and for their soft wool.

Mother sheep feeds hungry lambs

DAIRY FARMS

Dairy farms are busy places where you can see cattle being milked twice each day.

Most dairy farmers use electric milking machines. While being milked, the cows are loosely held in metal collars called **stanchions.**

Milk is removed from the farm by trucks. Later, it is sold in stores.

Farmers raise many **breeds,** or kinds, of cattle. Some breeds produce more milk than others.

Visitors making a new friend in the pasture

Raising pigs for the fair

Ducks are raised for meat and down

HORSE FARMS

Horse farms are well-known for their green pastures and bright, white wooden fences. But the main reason to visit a horse farm is to see the horses themselves!

Horse farms may raise riding, racing or work horses. Work horses, like the Belgian breed, have thick, heavy bodies. Riding and racing horses are slimmer.

Horse farms hire **trainers** to teach horses how to be ridden.

Standardbred foal was born to run

POULTRY FARMS

You can probably find a chicken or turkey farm nearby. Then you can see these noisy birds up close.

All poultry farms produce meat. Chicken farms, however, are also important for the eggs they produce.

The fine breast feathers **(down)** of ducks and geese are used to line pillows and warm clothing.

Tom turkey strutting

SPECIAL FARMS

You may be lucky enough to find an unusual and special farm to visit. Some of these unusual farms raise fish, foxes, rabbits, minks, llamas, bees or even ostriches.

Florida has special farms where alligators are raised. Many restaurants in Florida serve 'gator meat.

Alligators are also raised for their skins, which are used to make leather for purses, belts and shoes.

Alligator at an unusual Florida farm

CROP FARMS

You may visit a farm without any animals at all. Crop farms raise such things as corn, hay, wheat, vegetables, cotton, rice and fruits.

Orchards are crop farms where apples or cherries are raised. Groves are farms with oranges and grapefruit. Pine tree farms are sometimes called plantations.

Most crops are grown for people, but some are raised to feed farm animals.

Pumpkin crop in autumn

FARMS AT THE FAIR

Farmers attend fairs each summer or fall to show some of their finest animals and crops.

Visiting a fair, then, is like going to several farms at once! You can see row after row of prized animals and the farms' best fruits and vegetables.

Many farm animals are shown at the fair by school students. Members of the 4-H Club, for example, often raise livestock as a club project.

Glossary

breed (BREED) — Within a closely related group of farm animals, a certain type, such as Guernsey cattle

combine (KAHM bine) — a common type of harvesting machine used on farms

crop (KRAHP) — the yearly harvest of a particular kind of food plant, such as corn

domestic (duhm ES tik) — tamed and raised by people

down (DOWN) — the fine, soft breast feathers of ducks and geese

livestock (LIVE stahk) — domestic animals, such as cattle, sheep and hogs

poultry (POLE tree) — domestic chickens, turkeys, ducks and geese

ranch (RANCH) — a large farm, especially for cattle, in the West and South

stanchion (STAN shun) — a metal collar used to loosely hold cattle in a barn

trainer (TRAY ner) — one whose job is to teach, or train, certain actions to animals

INDEX